Praise for Sergeant Curtis
and the *7 Second Blackbelt's 77 Scenarios*

"Sergeant Curtis' intuition is different than yours and mine!"
—National Geographic Channel

"This book contains exactly the type of scenarios that I use to train new officers. It is incredibly effective and Chris is the best person to present it."
—Officer J. Rivera
Field Training Officer, Las Vegas Metropolitan Police Department

"As a DEA Agent, I have to be prepared to handle any type of situation that comes my way. Sergeant Curtis' 7 Second Blackbelt scenarios mirror the type of training I role-play in my mind everyday."
—Special Agent F. Contreras
Drug Enforcement Administration, DEA

"When I was attacked, I had no idea that something like this would ever happen to me. If I had a book like this back then, I could have had a plan. Sergeant Curtis has given me so much confidence with his training."
—Evelyn S.

"As a father, there is no worse nightmare I can imagine than someone harming my wife or son. This book gave me the peace of mind that we can be prepared."
—Isaac N.

"I have trained and operated worldwide. Of all the deadly force situations I have been involved in, I have learned one thing: Train. Sergeant Curtis knows his stuff."
—Salvatore Mascoli
Renowned Police/Military Trainer and Close-Combat Expert

"When a child goes missing, it's a race against time to find them. 7 Second Blackbelt is the type of training that could make a difference in a critical situation—a difference that could save a life."
—John Guydon
CEO, Lassy Project

"Your training was fantastic and ideally suited to the audience."
—U.S. State Department Expert Speaker Program Rep.

THE 7 SECOND BLACKBELT'S

77 SCENARIOS

SERGEANT CHRISTOPHER CURTIS (RET.)

THE 7 SECOND BLACKBELT'S 77 SCENARIOS

Introduction

"How would you handle a possible crime in progress?"

This book contains 77 real-life scenarios that have been encountered by people during the commission of crimes. Some of the scenarios are common, others not so much. Either way, with hindsight, those involved in the situation would have likely done something different had they known what was going to happen.

Now, you are being granted the luxury of seeing these situations in a non-threatening, safe environment. By reading and thinking through the incidents, you will be better prepared if you encounter one of them in the future.

The **7 Second Blackbelt** is the creation of Retired Police Sergeant, Christopher Curtis. Sergeant Curtis' career in law enforcement spans over twenty-five years. He traveled the world during his military service in the United States Marines and has been involved in multiple deadly force situations. As a lifetime martial artist and crime fighter, he has always had a fascination with ensuring that people feel safe. Several years ago, he created what he calls, the 7 Second Blackbelt.

The Blackbelt in the martial arts community is the highest level of achievement that a marital artist can attain. The philosophy of 7 Second Blackbelt is that a blackbelt exists inside of all of us. Our instinct and intuition are constantly working to protect us. We are born with a blackbelt when it comes to protecting ourselves.

The challenge many people face is that they are being conditioned to train too little, trust too much, and fear too often. This way of thinking is contrary to our true nature. The 7 Second Blackbelt brings you back to your natural state of oneness with your intuition.

7

Sergeant Curtis on the 7 Second Blackbelt

In my profession, people often ask me, "Is this area safe?" This was always a dilemma, because what people really want to know is whether the area is statistically safe. Then, they will decide by the number how safe they feel. There is an inherent challenge with this model of thinking. If you are the 1 in 1000 person (based on statistical data for the area) who is the victim of crime, then the area is unsafe to you and anyone else with whom you share your experience. If you base your feelings on statistical data, most places you visit are pretty safe. In fact, the odds of you becoming the victim of a violent crime are pretty low. However, in real life, you could be that one.

The 7 Second Blackbelt decreases the chance of you becoming that one. What I love most about the 7 Second Blackbelt is that it is truth. It is your natural state of being. Your brain wants to do nothing more than to protect that vessel you call you. For the most part, the 7 Second Blackbelt is about cognition and awareness. Listening to your intuition and being proactive when a threat is detected is the core of the intuitive blackbelt. Using a seven second window of tracking and acting if necessary, we can avoid violent acts planned against us or thrive in unavoidable crisis situations.

7 Second Blackbelt Conditions

The 7 Second Blackbelt teaches that the safest way to go about your day is to operate in 3 conditions.

The first condition is **Zone**. Zone is the most common of all the conditions. This is when we are engaged in an activity and the surrounding stimuli are completely or partially zoned out. We spend much of our day in this condition. It is very healthy to spend quality time in Zone. We should, however, understand that we all need balance. One

7

of the most common examples of Zone is walking down the street and talking on a cellular phone. I have interviewed criminals who say they often choose victims because they are "zoned out" on a mobile device.

> **Condition Zone**: The cognitive state of subconscious or singular connection. In this state, one is unaware of detectable stimuli (i.e. daydreaming, engaged in a phone call without multitasking).

The next condition is **Track**. This is the condition in which we sense stimuli and begin to track it for threat assessment. Upon finding that the stimuli are not a threat, we reengage our previous business. An example of Track, is when you are dining in a restaurant and a person walks in the door. Or, when you are reading and you hear a sound, stop to make sure it is not a threat and then go back to reading.

One day, I was sitting in my car in the parking lot. My daughter was about six at the time and I had already taught her these conditions. She was in her car seat in the back. I started talking to her about something and she was not answering me. So, I turned around and asked her why she was not responding. She was looking out of the car window and said, "Hold on Dad, I'm tracking this guy that is coming up to the car." That's my girl!

> **Condition Track**: The cognitive state of heightened awareness to stimuli.

The third condition is **On**. This condition is often instinctual. Our brains act without planning. Being startled and jumping back is a common example of an On response. We can train ourselves to be more proficient at protecting ourselves by training for crisis type situations. When not an instinctual response, On is thought out and planned. Effective tracking and threat assessment gives you the tactical advantage in most situations.

On is the easiest condition to identify. When it is instinct based, there is usually a jump or bracing when startled. And when it is planned, there is often a quick attack or assault. There is the guy that jumps out and scares you and gets the reflex punch or the bully that corners you and narrows your options and you choose to blast him in him the jaw before he hits you.

> **Condition On**: The instinctive response of fight, flight, freeze, appease or the planned action to a perceived threat.

These three conditions all have their purpose. A healthy mind can flow between these conditions as needed. I often find myself sitting in a restaurant working on my computer. The door to the restaurant opens and I make a quick assessment of the person entering. The moment that I feel this person is no threat, I get my head back into whatever I was doing. There is a cadence to this method of operation. My brain is so accustomed to shifting in this manner it requires very little thought.

Sergeant Curtis on Fear

Fear is natural and it is an extremely effective motivator. The key is to not allow it to paralyze you. Fear, like fire, can be an asset, if controlled, and a liability, if uncontrolled. Don't live your life in fear. Also, don't ignore the feeling of fear when it presents itself. There are many techniques you can use to calm yourself down in a critical situation. Proper breathing is the easiest, safest, and most effective.

May 2012
0330 hours

An example of controlling fear can be found in a call I went on as a police officer. I arrived on the scene of a convenience store robbery. I walked into the store and met the clerk, a young female in her early 20's. She was working the nightshift by herself. When I walked over to her, she was going over the receipts at the register. She calmly explained to me that the suspect entered the store and without warning, pulled a sawed shotgun from his jacket, pointed it directly between her eyes and ordered her to empty the register. She did and he fled. She told me the story as if she was giving me a recipe for her favorite dish. She wasn't upset or shaken, at all. She told me she expected that at some point she would get robbed. She planned in her mind how she would remain calm and comply with the robber's request. And, she did just that. For her, that technique worked. Most people placed in that situation, do not react that calmly. I reviewed the surveillance video and it happened exactly as she said. She was smooth, calm and collected throughout the entire incident. On another occasion, the same suspect shot another clerk that freaked out and could not open the register.

Sergeant Curtis on Training

When most people think of training, they think of a formal, structured setting and it turns them off. It does not have to be that way. Some of the best training is "what if" type training you conduct inside your head or with another person.

I served ten years as a Field Training Officer. Whenever I had "downtime" with my trainees, I would present them with scenarios. "What if, while we are sitting here eating dinner, that guy over there pulls out a gun and attempts to rob the place?" Or, "See that little kid that just got off of the school bus? What would you do if that guy driving that red pickup truck snatched the kid and drove off?"

Cops should be doing this kind of thinking all the time. As non-law enforcement, it should not occupy so much of your time, but occasionally you should play out scenarios in your head of what you would do and assess your options.

7

While in Roll Call as the Sergeant, I was responsible for conducting the briefing. During the entire month, we were having a rash of residential burglaries in this particular neighborhood. As I briefed the officers, I presented the scenario of them conducting a car stop in this target neighborhood that was getting hit by the burglar. The driver of the vehicle is the suspect in the burglary and, as soon as the officer turns on the red lights, the suspect bails from the car. Every officer participated and each had something positive to add to the potential situation. The next night, it actually happened, only it was the passenger that bailed and was taken into custody after a short foot pursuit. In debriefing, the officer that conducted the car stop thanked me and told me it was eerie how it felt like he had seen the incident play out in his head before and now it helped him perform at a higher level during the incident.

Sergeant Curtis on The Will To Win

For a short period in my career, I was a D.A.R.E. Drug Awareness Resistance Education Officer. I can remember parents would have a series of police-related questions on how to better protect their kids from illegal drugs. But, interestingly, parents were equally as inquisitive about protecting their children from being abducted or attacked. Very often, they would begin by saying something like, "My daughter weighs fifty-five pounds. How is she ever going to be able to fight off a grown man trying to kidnap her?" My response was, and always is, the same whenever I am presented with this type of question: "Let me put a ten pound cat in the corner of the room that does not want to be picked up and taken away. Then you go and try to put that cat in a bag." I would see the revelation wash over their face.

You see, it is not about size. It is about will. I have witnessed on hundreds of occasions the one with the will to win coming out victorious regardless of size or numbers. The cat is not negotiating whether or not it wants to be in the bag. The answer is no and it is non-negotiable. The cat will use every ounce of its power and every tool in its tool belt to make sure that it doesn't happen. That is how we must react when placed in a situation where we must decide. Do I get inside this person's van or not? If the answer is no, every fiber of my soul and my being backs this decision and it's ON.

Sergeant Curtis on Trusting Your Intuition

People often say to trust your intuition. Trusting your intuition is not usually the issue. The challenge is doing something proactive about what you feel.

Examples:
- Get out of the elevator, if the guy makes you uncomfortable.
- Take another route home.
- Break up with her or him.
- Get up to check that the door is locked.
- Check on your friend.
- Ask a trusted person to walk you to your car.

I am not saying to live your life in fear. What I am saying is: if you are in tune, alignment, and cadence with the universe, your intuition will speak to you.

One of the most effective tools used by police officers is a law based on intuition. In the United States of America, police are given the authority to conduct stops on people whose behavior appears to be reasonably suspicious to them.

These reasonable suspicion stops are based on a case that occurred in Cleveland, Ohio. The initial case, Terry vs. Ohio, involved detective Martin McFadden, a 35-year veteran police detective who was working in plainclothes. He observed three subjects acting in a manner that,

7

according to him, "didn't look right." Police often use the term JDLR, which stands for "Just Don't Look Right." While he observed no crime, he conducted a stop and recovered a pistol concealed on John Terry.

Detective McFadden later testified that he had developed routine habits of observation over the years and that he would "stand and watch people or walk and watch people at many intervals of the day." Scientists today refer to this as Expert Intuition. Detective McFadden went on to articulate the specifics of what caused him to be suspicious of Terry and his two counter-parts behavior. In legal circles, these inter-actions are referred to as Terry Stops or Stop and Frisk. While the offi-cer has witnessed no crime, a behavior or series of actions piques the officer's interest and they may, by law, stop this person and investigate. I have conducted thousands of these stops over the course of my career. The purpose here is not to discuss the particulars of Terry vs. Ohio, rather the application of observation of behavior that seems "not right" to us and our detection and response to this behavior.

For the 7 Second Blackbelt, people displaying this behavior are referred to as GMA's, which stands for "Gets My Attention." And you do not have to be a police officer to get that GMA feeling from a sit-uation.

I have witnessed multiple "in-progress crimes" in person, in real time, and have viewed hundreds of videos of these types of events. What I find most fascinating is not the act itself, but the behavior of the sus-pect prior to committing the crime. In my study of this behavior, I have noticed that human behavior amongst criminals, even across cul-tural lines, remains fairly constant. Most criminals exhibit the same or similar mannerisms prior to the event. Most police officers can identify this type of behavior very quickly, because, through training and expe-rience, they are keyed in to detect these mannerisms.

I assigned a name to this behavior. I call it Signs of Suspicion (SOS). The signs of suspicion are commonly brought on by stress when a per-son is about to commit a crime or an act of violence. This is called anticipatory stress. The person about to commit the crime is antici-pating the act and this causes them a level of stress. They reveal their

7

hidden intention through micro expressions with their face and body language. Body language is incredibly articulate, if you "listen." When tracking or observing behavior, you should always be acutely aware and internally inquisitive of the person's true intention for engaging you. Human behavior, for the most part, should feel and be natural when engaged by strangers.

This is a list of some of the most common SOS behaviors. While none of these mean that a person is about to commit a crime, they should alert you. Remember, this is but one piece of the entire picture.

SOS- Signs of Suspicion:
- Adjusting clothing
- Animated gestures
- Happy feet (inability to stand still)
- Area scanning
- 1000-Yard Stare
- Grooming
- Stretching
- Heavy/deep breathing
- Heavy perspiration
- Yawning
- Contorted body movements and/or positions
- Any form of concealment: hands/items
- Intentional body dialogue between others
- Unusual response to a question
- Persistence
- Uncomfortable eye contact or lack of eye contact
- Directional or positional changes acute/multiple times
- Placing hands on face or head
- Repeating your comment or response
- Ignoring you
- Entering an establishment-leaving-reentering
- Directing unnatural attention to a mobile device

7

Enhancements to behavior:

- Hats
- Gloves
- Sunglasses
- Hoods
- Masks
- Bandanas

Often, it is challenging to verbally articulate these behaviors, but the mind can read danger. In conjunction with other factors, identifying these mannerisms can act as a warning signal to you. The totality of the circumstances matter! For the most part, these behaviors singularly, and independent of any other indicators are usually benign. However, trust your intuition!

7

Rules

The rules to this book are simple. Respond to the scenario with a detailed answer on how you would handle the situation. Two follow-up questions are allowed from the responder, if clarification is needed. The person asking the question creates the follow-up response to the question.

Discuss your answers after, so you can create clear plans in your mind of how you will respond if confronted in one of these scenarios in real life. Play it out in your mind. Really envision how it will play out, with you as a thriver and not a victim. Remember—if you play it in your mind, as far as your brain is concerned, you have done it.

Sample Scenario and Response
You wake up to see an intruder climbing in the window next to your bed.

Response
I would quietly grab my phone and call 911. I would then grab my baseball bat and scream for the person to get out of the house.

Follow up question from responder for clarification
Does the person keep coming in?
"Yes."
I would then starting beating the intruder with the bat.

2nd Follow up question from responder for clarification
Do they keep coming in?
"No."
Then, I would stop and lock myself in the bathroom.

Now, discuss the pros and cons of this response. If you are alone, just think through the pros and cons.

7

The above response is not mine and, as a law enforcement professional, I could provide some constructive feedback as to why I might do things differently. It does not make the above response wrong. It just provides ideas that may assist others. I have a saying: "Let the results be the judge."

An example of constructive feedback for the above scenario could be to grab the bat and phone, simultaneously. Maybe start screaming as soon as you see the intruder, as to startle them and alert neighbors. Or possibly fleeing the residence to a neighbor may be better than locking yourself in the bathroom.

Many of the 77 Scenarios were created by using real-life situations that I encountered as an officer. These scenarios are intended to be an incubator for discussion. Most of the time, there is no one right answer. Collectively, you should talk about the specifics of your home, life and situation that make your answer right for you.

Remember, your answers should be comprehensive. Start with more and then think through the totality of the circumstance. Cut out what doesn't work, and add what will.

7

➡ THINGS TO CONSIDER

When it comes to scenarios, they can be incredible enhancements to self-training. As a professional in the field of personal safety, I look at these scenarios through a different prism than most people.

In order to assist you in your decision making process, I have added a series of informational "bullets" that I refer to as, "Things to Consider."

These "Things to Consider" are factors you may want to use to assist you in making your decision.

Remember, every situation is different, and hopefully you are never placed in one of these scenarios; but, if you are, you will then be better prepared to take the correct action for the exact set of circumstances you encounter.

As a disclaimer, this book is not a "how to" step-by-step procedural manual on how to handle critical incidents. It is a book to get you thinking. So, if you are placed in a situation, your mind will operate more fluidly.

77 SCENARIOS

"I COULD ALWAYS SPOT MY PREY WHEN I WAS ON THE HUNT. IF THEY SPOTTED ME FIRST, IN MY MIND, THEY WERE NO LONGER PREY."

—Three-time convicted ex-felon, Swoo Jackson

J.D.L.R
(JUST DON'T LOOK RIGHT)

—Police terminology

"HALF OF WHAT YOU SEE, NONE OF WHAT YOU HEAR."*

—Old police maxim
Multiple author attributions

"TAKE CARE OF THE MISDEMEANORS, AND THE FELONIES TAKE CARE OF THEMSELVES."

—Old police maxim

7

<u>ONE</u>

You arrive home from shopping to find your front door ajar. You are sure you locked it and no one is supposed to be inside your home.

Response:

_____

_____

_____

_____

_____

_____

_____

> ➡ **CONSIDER THIS**
>
> Turning on lights can allow you to scan a room.

<u>TWO</u>

You pull up to a stoplight and a stranger approaches your passenger side window. The window is rolled up and they are attempting to speak to you.

Response:

_____

_____

_____

_____

_____

_____

7

THREE

You are about to enter a convenience store and you see a person at the counter yelling at the clerk. The clerk appears startled.

Response:

_____

_____

_____

_____

_____

_____

_____

➡ CONSIDER THIS

Intervening in a third party situation can sometimes turn an attacker's attention on to you.

FOUR

A young child approaches you on the street and tells you they are lost.

Response:

_____

_____

_____

_____

_____

_____

_____

FIVE

You are driving on a poorly lit, desolate street stopped at a red light. A car edges up and taps you from the rear. You are unhurt and you see the male driver exit and begin to walk up to your driver-side window.

Response:

_____

_____

_____

_____

_____

_____

_____

7

SIX

You see a person peering into your neighbor's window.

Response:

_____

_____

_____

_____

_____

_____

_____

> ➡ **CONSIDER THIS**
>
> 911 systems can sometimes identify your location.

SEVEN

A male and female are engaged in what sounds like and appears to be a domestic related shoving match in the middle of the street.

Response:

_____

_____

_____

_____

_____

_____

_____

7

While shopping at a hardware store, you hear gunfire a few aisles over.

Response:

_____

_____

_____

_____

_____

_____

_____

> ➡ **CONSIDER THIS**
>
> Hiding is sometimes a better option.

A person snatches your mobile phone from your hand while you are walking down a populated city street.

Response:

_____

_____

_____

_____

_____

_____

_____

7

While seated at a bus stop, you notice a middle-aged man standing nearby, inching towards you.

Response:

> ### ➡ CONSIDER THIS
>
> A baseball bat or similar object used as a personal defense tool requires space to swing.

ELEVEN

You are awoken, in the middle of the night, to the sound of a window breaking inside your home.

Response:

7

TWELVE
While at home, you hear the sound of a woman screaming some-where in the vicinity.

Response:

_____

_____

_____

_____

_____

_____

_____

➡ CONSIDER THIS

Writing down a license plate is a great way to provide witness information.

THIRTEEN
While driving, you see a woman seated in the backseat of the car next to you screaming. The male driver acts as if nothing is going on.

Response:

_____

_____

_____

_____

_____

_____

7

While walking down the street, you turn to see a subject in the process of picking your pocket.

Response:

_____

_____

_____

_____

_____

_____

_____

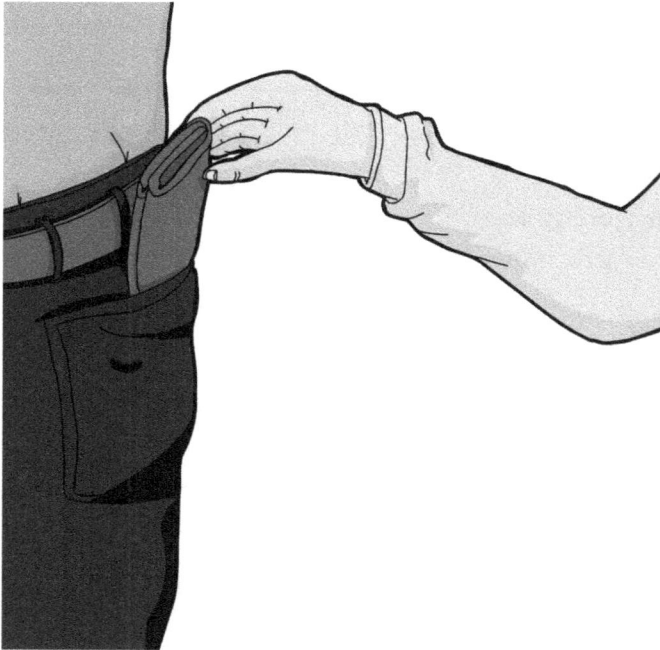

7

FIFTEEN

Upon exiting the store, you see a person pulling on the door handle of your car in the parking lot.

Response:

_____

_____

_____

_____

_____

_____

_____

SIXTEEN

A boy that appears to be ten years old rings your doorbell at midday. Through the peephole, you see he appears to be crying.

Response:

_____

_____

_____

_____

_____

_____

_____

7

SEVENTEEN

A person you identify as your neighbor comes to your front door banging and screaming for help.

Response:

_____

_____

_____

_____

_____

_____

_____

➡ CONSIDER THIS

Creating buffer space between you and someone approaching can increase your ability to react.

EIGHTEEN

You arrive home from work. You unlock your door and find an intruder inside your house and you are face-to-face.

Response:

_____

_____

_____

_____

_____

_____

_____

NINETEEN

While walking to work, you sense a person following you on foot. You turn and see nothing, but the feeling is still very strong.

Response:

_____

_____

_____

_____

_____

_____

_____

7

TWENTY

An irate male approaches you on a street screaming incoherently.
Response:

_____

_____

_____

_____

_____

_____

_____

TWENTY-ONE
You are walking out of a convenience store, as a man walks in with a bloody nose. He tells you that there is a "crazy guy" outside that just ran up and punched him.
Response:

_____

_____

_____

_____

_____

_____

_____

7

TWENTY-TWO
While walking down the street, a car traveling in the same direction pulls close to the curb and asks you for directions.

Response:

_____

_____

_____

_____

_____

_____

_____

➡ CONSIDER THIS

A person nearby can also be an accomplice.

TWENTY-THREE
You turn the corner, while walking down a city street, and find two males beating an elderly male that is lying on the ground.

Response:

_____

_____

_____

_____

_____

_____

_____

7

TWENTY-FOUR

While waiting for an elevator, a male arrives and stands to wait for the same elevator. You feel uncomfortable about this person.

Response:

_____

_____

_____

_____

_____

_____

_____

➡ CONSIDER THIS

Pepper spray, used in close quarters, can have an adverse affect on you and responding emergency personnel.

TWENTY-FIVE

While walking down the street at night, you see, in the distance, about a block away, five young males walking in your direction.

Response:

_____

_____

_____

_____

_____

_____

_____

7

TWENTY-SIX

You see a gun in the waistband of the person in front of you on line at a grocery store. Though covered by a shirt, you can tell that it is definitely a firearm.

Response:

_____

_____

_____

_____

_____

_____

_____

➡ CONSIDER THIS

Just because you are shot, does not mean you are going to die.

TWENTY-SEVEN

You sense the car behind you is following you on your drive to work.

Response:

_____

_____

_____

_____

_____

_____

_____

7

TWENTY-EIGHT

You arrive home to find your garage door open. You are *sure* you closed it.

Response:

_____

_____

_____

_____

_____

_____

_____

➡ CONSIDER THIS

You can destroy a crime scene by being nosey.

TWENTY-NINE

You arrive home to find your garage door open. You are *unsure* you closed it.

Response:

_____

_____

_____

_____

_____

_____

7

THIRTY

While jogging in the park, you see two people engaged in a sexual act in the backseat of a car.

Response:

_____

_____

_____

_____

_____

_____

_____

THIRTY-ONE

While walking on a city street, a person approaches you with an offer to sell you a high-end cellular phone at a huge discount.

Response:

_____

_____

_____

_____

_____

_____

_____

7

THIRTY-TWO

When leaving a department store, a young male snatches your bag and runs.

Response:

_____

_____

_____

_____

_____

_____

_____

7

THIRTY-THREE

You see a male is walking away from a female that is yelling at him and cursing at him. It appears to be a domestic dispute. She begins to yank at his shirt and slap the back of his head.

Response:

_____

_____

_____

_____

_____

_____

_____

THIRTY-FOUR

You see a toddler locked inside of a car in the parking lot of a convenience store.

Response:

_____

_____

_____

_____

_____

_____

_____

7

THIRTY-FIVE

While driving down the street at lunchtime, a woman runs up to your driver-side window and begins banging on it. She is screaming incoherently.

Response:

_____

_____

_____

_____

_____

_____

_____

THIRTY-SIX

You pull up to a drive-up ATM. You begin your transaction and see a male subject walking up to your car from the rear.

Response:

_____

_____

_____

_____

_____

_____

_____

7

An unmarked car with police lights pulls behind you, as you are driving home from an evening movie. The driver activates their lights and siren indicating for you to pull over. This is a desolate road.

Response:

> ➡ **CONSIDER THIS**
>
> Fighting is sometimes a better option.

THIRTY-EIGHT

You get into your car, start the engine, and a stranger appears from the backseat.

Response:

7

THIRTY-NINE

You are at home and you hear you neighbor's home alarm activate.
Response:

_____

_____

_____

_____

_____

_____

_____

7

FORTY

As you are pumping gas at the gas station, three subjects approach you. They are together and ask if you can spare change.

Response:

_____

_____

_____

_____

_____

_____

_____

➡ CONSIDER THIS

911 systems can sometimes misidentify your location.

FORTY-ONE

You arrive home to find an intruder rummaging through your closet. They do not notice you.

Response:

_____

_____

_____

_____

_____

_____

_____

7

While sitting in your living room, you hear what you believe to be several gunshots a few houses away.

Response:

> ➡ **CONSIDER THIS**
>
> Police officers sometimes misidentify victims for suspects and "friendly fire" has killed more than a few innocent people.

FORTY-THREE (A)

You see a middle-aged *woman* pulling a screaming toddler into a car.

Response:

7

FORTY-THREE (B)

You see a middle-aged *man* pulling a screaming toddler into a car.
Response:

_____

_____

_____

_____

_____

_____

_____

FORTY-FOUR

On a crowded city street, a woman drops a handful of coins in front
of you.
Response:

_____

_____

_____

_____

_____

_____

7

During your lunch break from work, a teenage girl approaches you while walking down the street and asks you for change for a dollar.

Response:

FORTY-SIX

While walking down the street, you collide with a person unintentionally. They drop a phone and claim you are responsible for replacement cost.

Response:

7

FORTY-SEVEN

A teenage girl approaches you on a busy city street and asks to use your cellular phone to call her mom to pick her up.

Response:

┌───┐
➡ CONSIDER THIS

Screaming can sometimes cause an assailant to flee.
└───┘

FORTY-EIGHT (A)

A female co-worker tells you she is going through a very contentious break-up. She asks you to walk her to her car after work because she is afraid.

Response:

7

FORTY-EIGHT (B)

You choose to walk her, and when you get to the parking lot you see the male standing next to her car.

Response:

_____

_____

_____

_____

_____

_____

_____

7

You approach your car, after shopping, and notice a knife with what appears to be blood on its blade on the sidewalk next to your car.
Response:

_____

_____

_____

_____

_____

_____

_____

➡ CONSIDER THIS

Night blindness is real and night vision adjustments greatly affect accuracy when using a weapon.

FIFTY (A)

After leaving a *concert* late in the evening, you notice a male attempting to walk an extremely intoxicated and nearly unconscious female away from the venue.
Response:

_____

_____

_____

_____

_____

_____

_____

7

FIFTY (B)

After leaving a *bar* late in the evening, you notice a male attempting to walk an extremely intoxicated and nearly unconscious female away from the venue.

Response:

_____

_____

_____

_____

_____

_____

_____

FIFTY-ONE

While walking by a business, you notice that the interior is engulfed in flames. The elderly storekeeper is screaming that her granddaughter is still inside.

Response:

_____

_____

_____

_____

_____

_____

_____

7

A U.S. postage-paid letter arrives at your home addressed to you. You open it and it is a profession of love from a complete stranger.

Response:

_____

_____

_____

_____

_____

_____

_____

➡ CONSIDER THIS

Calling 911 and remaining silent can be an effective way to transmit location and information to a police dispatcher.

FIFTY-THREE

You are at a wedding party for a friend. An intoxicated guest is attempting to leave in their car and they are visibly incapable of driving.

Response:

_____

_____

_____

_____

_____

_____

7

A recently fired employee from where you work is pacing before the front door of your place of employment. You have always had a strange feeling about this person.

Response:

_____

_____

_____

_____

_____

_____

_____

FIFTY-FIVE

An ex has left a bouquet of dead flowers at your front door.

Response:

_____

_____

_____

_____

_____

_____

_____

7

FIFTY-SIX
An elderly man runs up to you bleeding profusely from the head yelling, "They just robbed me, please help me."
Response:

> ➡ **CONSIDER THIS**
>
> No one is better at protecting you than you.

FIFTY-SEVEN
You discover that your passenger-side tires are flat, as you enter your car to drive to work.
Response:

7

You get a call from your significant other. They just arrived at home and found a strange car in the driveway.

Response:

_____

_____

_____

_____

_____

_____

_____

➡ CONSIDER THIS

Screaming can sometimes cause an assailant to identify your location.

FIFTY-NINE

A new neighbor moves onto your street. They have a party that goes well past midnight with loud music. You look out the window and see several intoxicated people being rowdy and yelling.

Response:

_____

_____

_____

_____

_____

_____

_____

7

SIXTY

You are awakened by your dog barking aggressively. It appears they sense something.

Response:

_____

_____

_____

_____

_____

_____

_____

7

As you turn the corner when walking into a store, you see a very large male punch a female in the face and run.

Response:

_____

_____

_____

_____

_____

_____

_____

SIXTY-TWO

You exit a store after shopping and in front of you there is a group of teens bullying a much younger girl. Their actions consist of verbal taunting, pushing, and other forms of physical aggression.

Response:

_____

_____

_____

_____

_____

_____

_____

7

You notice what appears to be a twelve-year-old girl very intoxicated on a street corner drinking wine.

Response:

_____

_____

_____

_____

_____

_____

_____

➡ CONSIDER THIS

Police officers are human and sometimes make mistakes.

SIXTY-FOUR

While inside a convenience store, you notice a police officer attempting to take a shoplifter into custody. The suspect is fighting and getting the best of the officer.

Response:

_____

_____

_____

_____

_____

_____

7

You witness a car accident occur in front of you. The at-fault driver starts to drive away.

Response:

_____

_____

_____

_____

_____

_____

_____

> ### ➡ CONSIDER THIS
> Video/Audio recordings and pictures make great evidence.

You just finished filling your car with fuel at a multi-pump gas station. There are several other people filling their cars, as well. You see a man pull a purse from the window of the car next to him. A young boy sitting inside the car yells and chases after him.

Response:

_____

_____

_____

_____

_____

_____

_____

7

SIXTY-SEVEN

While shopping in a department store, approximately 20 people walk in together. They begin filling bags with clothing. They are giving each other hand signals.

Response:

_____

_____

_____

_____

_____

_____

_____

SIXTY-EIGHT

While inside the gym, you notice a person checking locks to see if they are secure.

Response:

_____

_____

_____

_____

_____

_____

_____

_____

7

SIXTY-NINE

You turn the corner on a city street and come face-to-face with a male holding a knife to another man's throat. They both turn and see you.

Response:

_____

_____

_____

_____

_____

_____

_____

➡ CONSIDER THIS

Fleeing is sometimes a better option.

SEVENTY

A person that is driving behind you is angry at the way you are driving. You notice hand gestures from them in your rearview mirror. At the stoplight, they pull in front of you to block you from going forward and start screaming at you.

Response:

_____

_____

_____

_____

_____

_____

_____

SEVENTY-ONE

While on vacation, an aggressive panhandler follows you and won't take no for an answer.

Response:

_____

_____

_____

_____

_____

_____

_____

7

You walk out to your car and suddenly hear bloodcurdling screams next to you. You turn to see a large dog mauling a seven-year-old girl.

Response:

_____

_____

_____

_____

_____

_____

_____

➡ CONSIDER THIS

Fleeing from an attacker on foot onto a busy street full of traffic can be deadly.

A teenage boy approaches you on the street with your driver's license and says that your wallet was stolen. He has your license and asks for a reward.

Response:

_____

_____

_____

_____

_____

_____

_____

7

SEVENTY-FOUR

After shopping, you approach your car and find an envelope addressed to you under the windshield wiper. You open it to find a rambling letter professing love to you from a complete stranger.

Response:

_____

_____

_____

_____

_____

_____

_____

SEVENTY-FIVE

You are on an airplane sitting in a window seat and seated directly next to you is a large male. Mid-flight, he begins to talk to himself and mentions committing acts of violence upon other passengers.

Response:

_____

_____

_____

_____

_____

_____

_____

7

SEVENTY-SIX

You have a strange feeling about a co-worker. This person often speaks of doom and violent acts. On this day, they walk into work, clear their desk and say, "Today is the day." They then walk into the restroom.

Response:

_____

_____

_____

_____

_____

_____

_____

SEVENTY-SEVEN

Your neighbor knocks on your door and says her adult son is acting strange. He has taken off all of his clothes and is speaking of dying and hallucinating.

Response:

_____

_____

_____

_____

_____

_____

_____

Bonus

SEVENTY-EIGHT

You are walking down a city street and notice a man coaxing a ten-year-old boy into his car. They do not appear to know each other or to be related.

Response:

_____

_____

_____

_____

_____

_____

_____

7

OUTRO

There is no one foolproof method to combating crime. There are, however, many techniques and tactics to reducing your chances of being involved and increasing your ability to thrive in a critical incident. I choose not to use the word survive. Thriving is intention based. Surviving can happen by chance.

There is a black belt inside of all of us when it comes to protecting our loved ones and ourselves. One day, my daughter pointed to this 6′ 5″ muscle-bound guy and asked me, "Dad, can you beat him in a fight?" My response, "Depends on what we are fighting for."

Unleash the black belt in you.

Stay fit, stay informed, and train.

BONUS TIP

Being a good witness is always good advice. The simplest piece of information a person can gather is often overlooked—the license plate. And even when people do remember to note the license plate, they at times confuse the numbers or letters. An easy way to overcome this challenge and better remember the plate is to do what police officers do in these situations: use the police phonetic alphabet. Here it is. Learn it and share it with your family. You can even make it a game with your younger children. So 267AHT is Two, Six, Seven, Adam, Henry, Tom—Then say whatever state it is.

You brain recalls the plate easier because of the associated phonics.

7

THE POLICE PHONETIC ALPHABET

A- Adam
B- Baker
C- Charlie
D- David
E- Easy
F- Frank
G- George
H- Henry
I- Ida
J- John
K- King
L- Lincoln
M- Mary
N- Nora
O- Ocean
P- Paul
Q- Queen
R- Robert
S- Sam
T- Tom
U- Union
V- Victor
W- William
X- X-Ray
Y- Yellow
Z- Zebra

Sergeant Christopher Curtis (Ret.)
Crime Prevention Specialist, martial artist, and author

Christopher, AKA Sarge, is a New York City native. After graduating from high school, he enlisted the United States Marine Corps and was selected as the Honor Graduate of his platoon. Christopher conducted multiple operations in several countries in the Mediterranean. He subsequently attended MCESG Quantico, Virginia where he graduated with honors and went on to serve tours at U.S. Embassies- Belgrade, Yugoslavia, Caracas, Venezuela, and Asunción, Paraguay. After his honorable discharge he joined the ranks of the Las Vegas Metropolitan Police Department.

Christopher excelled quickly and worked in many sections of the police force. His twenty-year career highlights include his five years as a Hostage Negotiator, his Lifesavings Awards and his status as a finalist for National Officer of the Year 2013.

Christopher's other achievements include being a featured speaker for the Downtown Project Speaker Series, his frequent appearances on the COPS TV show, and being a Law Enforcement subject matter expert and frequent featured guest on the National Geographic hit television show "Brain Games." Curtis is a two-time published author, and highly sought after speaker in the U.S. Department of State Expert Speaker program. Sergeant Curtis is a CPTED Specialist and has evolved the science into his own creation of Embraceable Space. He stays active as a certified fitness trainer and creator of lovejitsu— the study of the relationship between love and the disciplines of martial arts. He is also the creator the "7 Second Blackbelt," an incredibly comprehensive course of study that teaches the student to become a trained observer.

Mr. Curtis has been involved in hundreds of critical incidents and shares his experience through his course.

Visit 7secondblackbelt.com for upcoming seminars and bookings.

Connect on LinkedIn: www.linkedin.com/in/downtownsarge

Follow on twitter @7secondblkbelt.